THE JESTER'S FOOTPRINT

A COLLECTION OF POEMS

BY
BECKA THOMPSON

for those who've known the haunting steps of love
and the quaking despair of grief
BT

THE JESTER'S FOOTPRINT BY BECKA THOMPSON

THE COMEDIES

THE RIVER:

Anyway, what am I saying?

> I'm saying I think you're amazing

and if
you don't have someone telling you that every day
that is a shame.
I'm saying you've intoxicated me and I don't know
how to sober up, nor do I want to.
I'm saying when the rivers of life keep moving,
sometimes you need to take the snapshot while you can,
while you're there,

> even if it comes out blurry:

Well, I'm here now,
looking at you,
and I know my futile attempts are blurry:
steeped in idol flattery
and benign hyperbole;

> but

they're just attempts
to capture a moment:
a moment in my own life and
hopefully
a moment in yours.

If I could
I would
buy you a drink and
write you a song and
sing of your restless beauty all night,
but I can't;
you're not here
i'm not there;

yet the river keeps moving...

> I'm not made of anything spectacular

but I do know a few things:

I know that one day nothing but my dust will remain
                          on this earth.
I know that I have very little to give anyone except for
the deep penetrations
of
my heart,
I know that sharing intimate quiet with someone else is the greatest
height of human relating.

                    It is rare and terrifying;
yet the terror is not malignant,
but rather borne of our deepest insecurities and desires.

I know that sometimes the universe of thought, matter and creation
gives us moments juxtaposed against the life we've lived;
and if we don't see those moments cast in that particular ecliptic light
we will miss the beauty of what is meant to be revealed to us.

                    My life is a story of a ship being steered
against the tide
and the moon
and all the other heavenly bodies
gently trying to coax me back onto course.

                    The clouds parted when you smiled
at me,
and it was no April Fools;
it was like looking into the face of God,
and knowing,
for the first time in so many long years;

which way to travel.

THE TOUCH OF ANGELS

I don't want to go.

I just want to breathe in the
Space
Where you are.
One more breath
And then another
And
Another.

... To be close to you.
ah…!
Something in my soul
Aches
Just to be close to you.

I cannot explain it.
Please don't ask.
It wouldn't make sense even if I could.

How can I make sense of this?
It was an instant,
A moment,
And the nexus of
My world
Came into focus.
I was a primal being
On the edge of an ancient society
First seeing a solar eclipse--
Could I prepare my eyes for what I was to see?
Could i predict it was coming?
Could I predict what you would do to my every pore?

But now I can't stop thinking
Hoping
Wondering
Charting--
When,
If ever,
Will it happen again...?
Will you happen again?

Like pagans sorting out the stars,
The journey will be long,
I'm sure,
To solving such an elusive equation;

But for here
And now
I can't get myself to leave...

Just one more breath
Under the light of heaven.

Just one more.

RED HAWK GETAWAY

There are three hawks circling the sky
And the migration
Of a different flock
Does nothing to quiet
Their splendor of the day.

The whispy white against a perfect blue
Outlines their form to my eye.

Oh that I could float away with them,
To cast myself onto their gale!
Yet I am earthbound
And can not barter my way
To their freedom

But even a land dweller has the gift of eyes
And the birds understood enough
To let me gaze.

MUSIC

The music of our lives
Holds such a tumultuous melody at times.
When the snare and timpani
Rule the thundering backdrop
And the horns are sounding
And the violins are in such fury
More than one instrument
Loses a string.

We wait for the bloody cursing to be over
For the soft refrain of the lone
Oboe to strike again;
For that was a gentle opus inside
The core of the madness that has now enveloped our ears.

Perhaps this symphony is by Grieg
And it only escalates to it's final
Triumphant
Death.
Or maybe it is Chopin
And it's brooding will return to something softer.

It is so difficult to tell which way the music will shift
When you have never before heard the verse.
But the pounding in your heart
Is escalating
Everything in your body
To such a nervous rant
That you pray
Soon
The solitary voice can be heard again
And the soft single solo
Call out to you from the back of the pit
And perhaps in that small chorus
It may be
your own voice
That you hear
Singing.

ETERNITY IN MY HEART:

The world is so vast and expandable.
What hope do any two people have of connection?
The ills and spills of a
Culture dying for order
Stigmatizes
The chaos of ourselves
And if you do not manage it correctly
You are caste.

Still your smile
Shines
In the starlight
And I hear you whispering my name
In the mud of my earthbound footprints.

They stride toward you.

Somewhere in the heavens you are tragically unreachable,
Yet my feet will not cease their motion
And my eyes will never stop looking up.

NOW

I wish to simply lay with you in the quiet
To wrap my body around yours
As the systems of the world
Pass around us:
The sun in its fix
Allowing the earth to spin past
And all the products
That essence manufactures;
Sunrise
Sunset
The moon desperately clinging to the earthly course
Causing the tides
To sway
And the light
Of the evening to
Swell--
Yet you and I would remain
Locked in an embrace
As mars
Rose to Venus
And Orion's belt
Wrapped itself
Past the dark side
To the dippers
And Cassiopeia
Would twinkle
On us just enough
To illuminate
The cusp
Of your curves.

And the wind would blow
And the trees would creak
And nothing else
Would interrupt us.

And your breathing
Would be a fixture
As a timepiece
For my heart

And I would measure it

And deny its rousing
For as long
As the light of
The heavens would allow.
Until you and I both
Were utterly
Satisfied.

TRIGONOMETRIC PARALLAX

Eternity stretches out before us
In the cold
And in the darkness;
But the trail wanders clearly
If you trust your footsteps.

I am a pauper of wit
And a wretch of humanity.
My soul yearns for that
Which it cannot craft;
And no amount
Of whispered thoughts
Into the black night
Will manifest them
Any sooner.

God in heaven must live
For I do.
If I take my thinking to have any merit, god must;
If I take my aching heart to have any value,
Then god must.
If I look into the expanse above me
I ponder the adventure
And breathe out a renewed pace,
Perhaps the creator of all
Will grant me serenity
When the light of my star
Finally Touches earth.

AWAKE WITH YOU

I raise my head
At an hour
Uncommon for me;
The birds are chirping
And there is a solace
In the rousing
Of the world.

You are conscious.
I know this;
On your feet
And at the helm
Of the healing
Of humanity's
Atrocities,
One suture at a time.

I wake myself
In an attempt
To understand
What simple pleasures
Are here with you,
That you may find comfort in
At the cusp of dawn...

The daylight is soft
And welcoming
As a safety
As a reminder
That through darkest fears
Light comes.

The canopy of earth is renewed

Every day this beauty sits,
Awakens in the quiet.
And you are there amongst it;
The squirrels
And robins
And red hawks

Peering for their first meal.
You are up with the aubade
And the cool dew
And the tunes of the
purple crowned
fairy wren
Celebrating the morning..

You spin in their midst
And become
One with the waking...

Like a cold creature
Warmed by the sun after
A long
And solitary night
You have drawn me up too.

Drawn me up to finding my own voice in the mist...

May I share my song with you
as you slip out of slumber
and gaze
with open eyes
the breaking
of the new world?

and
May the timber of my instrument
continue to
serenade you
until the darkness closes again?

Please?
There are only so many heartbeats left
Til the everlasting...

ROBERT'S PRAYER

What could I give you
You could not get yourself?
There is certainly a
Line of suitors
Looking
To grab hold
Of that spirit
Which has so enraptured me.

What could I possibly bring
That others could not already claim to you?

What do I have that no one else can possess?

I have my heart.
My mind.
The soul which cycles through the bones I animate.

What can a pauper pilgrim give a queen?
Perhaps a song.
Perhaps a lifetime
At your feet, clutching the hem of your footprint
As your jester
Your courtesan...

But could I nab you from heaven
And touch the scars on your heart
As an equal?

What can a broken bohemian
Give a goddess?

Perhaps some poetry

Perhaps.

TICKLE

I want to kiss your toes
I want to start my morning that way.
Then I'd rub your feet
Kiss your calves
And put my head
On your belly as you woke

Hopefully with a giggle.

Then I'd tip my head and smile at you
Stare at your beautiful face
Gaze into your eyes
Which fix me.

Would you entice me closer?

I want to kiss your fingertips
And give a healers hands
A
Healing touch

Let me stroke your porcelain arms
Strong and lean
And run my
Index finger
Along the crest of your collar
Until my hand can caress your
Face
Your face
Ah…
I want to kiss you!
I want to taste you.

And with a smile
I could tell you
How this has come to pass
All these things in my head

Let me love you.

It just starts with a little tickle in your toes…

I'll do the rest.

THE WOODPECKER

The world whispers on the doorstep of my mind
And all the words they would imbue upon my memory
Are but imprints in the sand...

But you chip into the stone of my heart
Until it has been tamed by your hand
And crafted by your soul.

I cannot resist what you shape by the firelight

When all others
Simply drive by,
You understand
That the greatest carver
Wields the craft
Not by might
Or nobility
But by
Every day
Stopping in the quiet of the woods

To leave a single etching.

EXPERIMENTS IN RECITATION

there is something
so transcendent
about bodies
and skin
and how they breathe
where there are two

we creatures
of the day
and night
linked
with the soil
of each other.

how to explain
how to explain
the unexplainable?

there is a mystery
to what happens
when you are near.
it is not like speaking
nor is it even like touch

it is part of the electromagnetic spectrum
you and I
we are.
we are waves
the energy we create

as if the tone of your being
harmonized with mine
and the
pulsing
vibrations
can be felt

like a passing storm

MY SWEET FRIEND

My sweet friend
I'm sorry I didn't know your suffering
I'm sorry I wasn't there to hold your hand
Kiss your forehead
Or rock your child to sleep
So you need not worry.
I'm sorry I didn't fight harder to span the space
That had come between us.
You were always teaching me
About bravery
Humility
And the power of a soft word.
I'm sorry I couldn't sing to you
When your own voice was getting tired.
I'm sorry I didn't celebrate you
As you did me
When your rings were exchanged.
Dear friend,
My beloved Toi,
Your smile was the last I saw
And not a scooter
But a kick ass Harley
Pulled you away.
It was a nice lunch and a
"See you later"
With a hug...

And indeed I will.
I will.

ODE TO A SUPERHERO

The tenderest smile
That the worlds ever known
He leaps tall building
And he's not yet Full grown

His heart is so full
I think at times It might burst
And the wealth of his joy
Can fill anyone's purse.

His name is of wonder
A child of the day
And he's made me ponder
The earth and our ways

He's changed every moment
I view dirt or sky
He's changed all the reasons
I give strength to try.

His voice is of sunlight
And his hugs forged from iron
The life that he tames
Makes the angriest, smile

His life is a poem
His face in a frame
And wherever god plants them
No one shares his name.

An honor I carry
The best prize I could own
To guide him to manhood
And call Patrick, my son.

DRAWN BY THE SURF

I draw lines in the sand
Darling
Ones meant for myself
Pictures
Of a person that never was...

You entered into me
And I cannot recover.

I draw pictures on the wall darling,
They are remnants of photographs
Etched into my memory
Of the ways of this fallen world,
I cannot abide...

I tasted you
And I cannot forget...

I write poems on the windows darling,
With my finger in the frost,
The cold is coming
We both feel it.
I write of distant ideas
And hopes
I write of dreams for another lifetime.

We breathed together
And I cannot take that cadence from my body.

In... out
In...
Out...

Life is fleeting.
Death comes to all.

But I touched you once
And you me
And at the very least--

We have that.

BURNING ALIVE

The fireside
Beckons me
Like an ever lively dance
I desire to join.

The hiss of its embers
Remind me that it is alive
Consuming
Breathing
In the oxygen
I need too.

We meet each other in the night
The cool
The darkness

And his fever feeds me.

Just past the grasp of my toes
The nimble flicker entices me.

Can I find the intonation of your rhythm?

The calm of the quiet stills
But still
You twist on
And dance until
Your appetite
Is filled.

CHASING WATERFALLS

I climbed up the inside of a waterfall today.

Really, I did.

But I did not make it far,
For it was slippery
And I knew that today
Was not
My day to die.

And though foolish
Do not worry,
I was not alone.
One friend was writing a story about it
Her duplicate book bag
Draped across a fallen log;
Another friend was
Singing the soundtrack of my folly;
Still a third was before me,
Climbing ahead,
Urging me on.

And when I got down
I stripped off my
Worldly weight
And got baptized
In the pools beneath.

It was no church baptism either.

There was no priest
Or font of marble
There was just me
The spirit of God
And the tumultuous
Thunder
Of the water.

A math nerd could probably calculate the rate it was falling,
And an anthropologist
Could ponder how we got here,

Either way the water
Was too strong
For me to keep my other burdens.

And I watched as they floated away
Down
The Little Caribou...

After being born again
I took it upon myself
To swim
-
For it was my preferred activity in my old life,
It my as well be in the new.

I sunned myself.
And the hemlock and
Evergreens
Applauded my nakedness.
For now I was back with them,
Raw and unimagined,
Of the earth
As I was meant to be,
Without the strange pageantry
And pomp
Crafted by men.

By the time
My breasts were warm
In the newness of my infancy
And my socks back on,
I had cried my last tear as one fearful of the passage.

My friends departed
Back into the wind
Where they now live.

And as I ascended
Up to the wandering trail
The roar
Of the water
Misted away
And the sweet tune
Of a single bird
Overtook my ears.

FOLLY STRIKES BACK

I cannot contain all that wells and swells in me.
Pertaining to you.
I dare not go too far too soon
Yet I want to
There is an urge in me to say all that is in me.
You are guarded.
I understand.
I wish I could get through the barricade.

Moonshine might do the trick.

I wish I could understand
The pains and heartbreaks you've been through
That I might soothe them.

I wish I could be one you would trust.
Though I have no right to that platform.

I wish I could know your mind.
You have great passions
And you manage them
Through walks and runs in the woods
Just like Henry David Thoreau
(But at a slightly faster pace)

I understand running away pain
And have feared so many times getting lost in the desert.
But there is hope in the moon
And healing in the sun

The little girl is still there
Underneath that toughness and fierce bravado.
And though you have undergone
The ways and means of life
You are she
Even still.

I wish to find you
Somewhere
Someday.

And the way you looked at me...
That way...
you looked at me...
Started this all.

The way you looked at me...
has bewitched my soul.

THE CARVER POET

The night falls around me
And this earthen veil
Cascades the moon
In darkness
And the swallows
Serendipitously
Know
To quench themselves before resting.
Why do not we?

This cloud ever blankets the mind.
I am in need of rest.

This broken vessel cheats us
In its inverses
How it grows strong before wise
And weak before usable
We falter.

I wish I were dancing in the moonlight.
Why do we allow ourselves to be trapped under this despair?

The minions want retribution
They want retribution for my failed attempts at revolution,
And I cannot quiet them
They do not tolerate
Different visions
And opines
And reasoned truth.

What is truth?

That question posed long ago
By a ruling regulator
To a condemned stone cutter
Has lingered in the air
Like a challenge
For centuries.

We're the apostles poets?

Jesus was.

He was the master builder
Master craftsman
And told tales with the best
Of the ancient storytellers.

Why are we afraid of stories?

I hope he visits me in my sleep tonight.
The insights he gives are unparalleled.

REFLECTIONS ON BECKS

I long to be known
And I long to know
Someone like you.

Someone who can set my heart ablaze
With a glance
Someone who can challenge my mind
With a word
Someone who can motivate my being
Just by animating theirs.

It doesn't take more than a blink
To realize
You're looking at something
You've never seen before;
But it takes a time uncertain
To convince your own uniqueness.

Is that even possible
When you have met one so utterly
Captivating?

No, I am not Prufrock nor was I meant to be.
I am a pauper on the Samaritans road
One meant for an allegory
To pity for the ages
Help guide a child
Or chide the wise.
Mine is a cautionary tale of mistrust and ruin...

Your light and beauty has swept into my life
Am I a fool to follow too quickly?
Or a fool to wait too long?
I have lingered at the doorstep of
Maidens and mermaids
And none has ever
Put my mind
To such a dizzying
Euphoria
Of confusion.

I breathe

And hope to smell you
I look
And hope to see you
I listen
And ache to remember your voice.

I cannot apologize enough
For the stupidity of my youth

Have you ever read that parable?
The hidden treasure in the field?
I will sell all that I have—

for someone like you.

I long to feel the soft lips
Of someone like you
Near to my ear
Perhaps whispering
Secrets
Of a childhood
In a coven of ninety eight men
With their changing voices
As their raucous humor.
But you and I can
Speak as initiates
On the fringe.

You skulk my thoughts
I can't help
But peer after you.

My heart is so heavy with the weight of my desire.

AN INSTANT MESSAGE

I want you
I want your fire
And your toil
I want your fears
And insecurities
I want the way you let go
To be me.

I want your spirit
And your anger
I want your sadness and frustration
I want the quiet moments that you seek
To be me.

I want your secrets
I want your fatigue
I want all the ways that you fail
To be mine.
I want to hold it all
And you
Every night
In my arms.

I want your passions
and all untamable
parts
I want all the ways that you run wild
to be me.

Your face could launch a thousand ships
and your body run a million miles;
But when the weather falls
There is just you.

And that

Is what I want.

ONE O'CLOCK

You are so beautiful
If you would but let me gaze on you
Until my final breath
I would live a life
Content
Until
one
of the
cancers of this world
takes me.

FIRST LESSON ON HOW TO BREATHE

A long time ago
I drove away from the madness
Of theory
And meritocracy,
Just for a day.

Just for a day, I set that aside
And for that
I was told I was crazy.

A long time ago
On a bright sunny morn
When no shadow was to be found
I wandered into a ballroom
Of the drake hotel
And for the first time
In many years
I pretended to be myself.

And after laughing and speaking
In my own voice
Walking into and out of a closet
I was given the
Greatest gift
I could ever receive:

An opportunity to forge friendships
Unlike any society
Condones.
Like a Walt Whitman poem
We lived in the company of fellows
With a love
Earned in the wars
And facing the fears
Of becoming
Who we already are.

My masks are many
And though my voice has faltered
Through the years

It still calls true
When one of my company
Is near.
I call for them
And they answer me.

There are so many ladders to climb and pools to jump into;
There is so much injustice of
Property
And birth;
But I have lived in the embrace
Of friendship
Forged in
The nights of running
And the daytime
Of drinking dreams.
I have stood on tables
And sung the heroes song;
One of beauty
And memory
And community.

I drove myself to Chicago one day
People thought I was crazy;
'Why would you go off on
An adventure
When tests
And rigor
And aptitude
Is to be measures against you?

What could possibly be worth
Such risk?'

I drove myself to Chicago one day
And walked into a ballroom of the drake hotel.
People thought I was crazy,
And I still am.

For if by crazy you mean
A lover
Or a poet
Or someone whose heart surges
Against the tide;
Then I am one;

And when I left the drake hotel
That day
I realized

I am not the only.

COME TO ME

Skin floats in the air
And cannot articulate
In sounds
What it expresses
In motion
Dangling
Posturing
Flesh

Intoxicating
The receiver.

Electrons
Protons
Neurons
Neutrons
Ions
Atoms
Adams
Apple
It wants to eat.

Hovering
Sensations
Waiting
To dissolve
Into breath.

Don't wait
Take it.

WINTER SOLSTICE

Quiet
And darkness
Some wine
And a fire
Cold air
Outside a warm room
And endless stars
Blanket the window.
The soft roar
Of a sleeping lake
And the frosty glare
Of the water

And a conversation
Or two
On a bed
With soft sheets
And warm pillows.

And the crackle of fire
Won't notice
When the words stop
And the soft sounds
Of the sweet
Communion
Of souls
Takes their place.
And the night would be endless
Endless peace
Endless comfort
Endless love
Under
A cloudless sky
So that heaven itself
Could peek.

RECOVERY

Your skin is as a bath
Of
Transitive
Euphoria.
The lightening
From your depths
Strikes me
In your fingertips
And I am immediately
Electrified.

THE JESTER'S EXPLANATION

Time stopped
When I realized
It was you I was seeing.

Like a hiccup in the great
Expanding omniverse
a wormhole,
a paradox,
It repeated itself in my mind.

I had to look again to be sure
But I never forget a face.

It was like a movie.
You know the movie--
Where the moron cracks little kid jokes
At the pig tail girl in braces
But then some years pass
And the moron sees the beauty
And cannot quite fathom

You smiled at me.

You smiled.

I did not deserve it.
And then something forbidden squeezed itself about my ribs.
It was that feeling you get when the sun shines on your intents but for a
moment:
Rapturous desire
And the thought
Of how to accomplish the goal
To accompany it.

You smiled at me.

I am the moron
And you were the kid sister of kid sisters.
But you have intoxicated me
And neither my brain
Nor body

Knows how to recover.

Am I now to blame if I then behave as
a Drunkard?
can I be faulted that I am drunk
On you?
If I play the jester
Oh queen?

THE TRAGEDIES

SIGH NO MORE, NONNY NONNY

i feel soft to the world
tragic almost—
though i wouldn't deign
to consider myself
worthy of such a title.
air flows beneath
my nose
and sifts effortlessly
into my sinews
yet can do nothing for my disposition.

i hurt people.

my mere existence does it.
my breathing.

the pain that wraps my
ribs
cannot be communicated to anyone
who has never experienced it

i blink
but no tears come
i choke
but no words
i shiver
yet cannot find the actions
to help
anyone
anything

i drown myself
in letters
and symbols
and distraction
hoping time can heal the wounds
i so endlessly
cut
by that air
that breathing
that existence
that

i am.

It is so hard
to look into another's eyes
and know
they do not see you.

i hope
the list of patients
needing remedy of me
does not
include
yourself.

FROZEN IN TWILIGHT

Dancing in the twilight
The sun sets
Yet again
For me and my efforts.
How long will the night linger?
The seasons change
And I do not have a means
To go south for winter.

I must hibernate against the winds
Of literature and podiums;
They are speaking
They are speaking of me
Even while I seek a conversation.

I will move my body
None the less,
For no one can stop the orbits of time
And I must ever sway to their precepts.
The winter is coming
Long and dark
But I will not be frozen
Forever.

DEATH OF A CHILD

Everything that was once good
About me
Is dead.

I no longer know joy
Or laughter
I cannot feel happiness.
All that was once fun
And carefree is now
Turned upside down and set ablaze
In the pyre
Of the ashes of hope.

Like Frodo,
Too long have I held the ring
Of managing your power
And I have forgotten the taste of bread
Or the feel of sunlight.

All that was once good within me
Is dead.

SOLVING THE SYSTEM

In the mist of light and certainty
I wish to call your name.
It is a hope
Laid on the mind of a fool;
And it grows in the garden of my years.

I have an affinity for the way time moves.
I feel it as the manner Einstein first perceived--
More like a wavy worm hole
Than a linear function.

Sail away with me.

I feel the wind blowing.

There is life outside the confines of our perception.
I am free
Yet ever lonely;
For still I need to unlock the cage of your heart.

NIGHT TIME FOR SINNERS

Night enters my consciousness
And it is filled with distant stars
The Sadness consumes me
For they are
Silent
And unreachable.

Time stops
And life
Dies around me.

All that remains
Is the electric pulse of my mind
And the
endless abyss
Of the
the cosmic eternity.

THE MOORS OF DESTITUTION

Life
Slips
So ruthlessly
Through our fingers
Through our hair
Through our late night brigades
Of song and dance
And early morning
Cups of coffee

Life wanders past us on the breeze
And we watch it
Haplessly
Unaware
It takes us along
Our years
Our moments

If we do not pause
To notice
Each other's heartbeats
It will be lost

There is so much chasing
After wind
Striving
For a fools errand.
And we put our hopes upon
Approval
Of witches
And elves
And other such
Fanciful
Stuff of our delusions into darkness.

And we hunger and
Thirst
But there is no bread to satisfy
Our longings
For how can bread fill the heart?

What sustenance can sate
The palate of the everlasting spirit?

Do not trifle your
Magnificent mind
With worthless things
Do not harbor and anchor
Your heart
On the moors
Of destitution

You are made of finer things.

There is no law against joy.
But
The world understands heartache.
It understands ruin.
And so we cling to that
Desperate to commune with our fellow man...

But like the pied piper
The children will come with the advent of music
And the breadcrumbs of song

Rise up to meet it.

In the night
Your space is far from mine
But in the light
I see you clearly...

And you are so beautiful.

GRADUATION TO GRASS

There is a soft whisper in the sky-
And it tells me of my humanity.
It is hard to decipher
At first
For the wind and the rustle of trees
Overcomes the quiet instruction.

Nature and nurture

Does it matter?
It is yet another device for us
To pass
The time,
To laud ourselves and
Confer notes of worthiness
With banners and tassels of gold and silver
Meant to stir up envy
And election
To our peers.

But the voice floating above the sky
Cares nothing for pomp
Or circumstance.
The voice that speaks out the heavens worth of wind
And caused the meteors which formed this land
Into their cataclysmic assault to sway;
Cares nothing for degree or podiums.

That voice which hovers above the depths of the sea
That voice is soft and deafening
And you cannot hear it
With your iPhone plugged in
Or your television on.
You cannot hear it
When you dwell in time outside of space.

I have been straining to let it rattle in my eardrums.

I used to believe that I was special
But the inverse
Of my argument

Ranked my fellows beneath me
As some predestined
Manifestation
Of my forebears righteousness
Alive in
ME.

And though we all build sky scrapers
To prove this is true in our own
Length of heart beats;
We know it is not.

The voice is not partial.
It hovers over us all.

I wish to hear it speak.
To sing a song.
To strike me with a fire
That burns forever
And never consumes.

There is a soft whisper in the sky
And it tells me of our humanity...

NIGHT SAILING

There is a solitude
And a specter
To the immensity
Which surrounds us
Consider the stars...

The crash of the never ending waves
Reminds me of the transient nature
of my innate purposelessness
In the cosmos.

They blow in and blow out
And there is no ceasing.

The whiskey I drink
Can warm me for a fortnight
But nothing more.

There is nothing more to me
But some breath and some
Bourbon.

I feel like a stargazer in my course
Led by the lights of the Infinite.

There is a boat on the horizon
Perhaps it is floating towards you.

My course is unknown
And I am wind blown...

Disappearing is so difficult.

COLLECTING SHELLS

I hate what you've done to me.

It is an evil sort of magic
That can cause one
To be so lovesick
That they can't enjoy
Their own celebration.

I'd rather sit on your porch
Discussing running shoes
Than party with the kings and queens of England
Or the rock stars
Of America
Or the athletes
Skulking the earth in their speed.

What have you done to me?

I am a shell of a human being.
The part of my heart
Which you consume
Grows and grows.
I wish someone could surgically remove
What you've started.
I could breathe free again.

There isn't enough distraction in the whole world
To stop this thing.

I hate what you've done to me.
Somehow
When I wasn't looking at all
And didn't even need the hassle,
You made me fall in love with you.
And you gave no consideration
To what you were doing;
No premeditation on your part
Or coaxing with lies;
But you did it all the same.
It's who you are.

You're just so....
Everything...
Everything good.

Don't get me started.

You should know, your ignorance of the situation is so frustrating.

I hate it almost as much
As I want you.

THE BATTLE OF JERICHO

I can't get you off of my mind

For so many years
We passed the same rooms
The same people
The same events.
We learned the same facts
From the same classrooms
And the same ideologies
Of the same professing
Scribes.

But we never shared
The same glance
At the same time
In the same direction.

Until that day.

We never shared
A Moment
Together

Until that moment.

You were there through every landmark of my youth
And I never noticed

But even fools at time get a second chance.

I can't get you off of my mind
And I don't want to.
You're so beautiful.
I'm So utterly unstable in my footing.
So foolish and fumbling in my attempts.

I want to do everything right.
I can't get you off of my mind
It is a struggle to try

it is a struggle
a fight...

I intend to lose.

THE OPEN DOOR

The slow dissent into the noise of night
The agony of the futility of reason
Smacks me over the earlobes again
And a raging bull
Next to me
Reminds me ever
That this folly lies too
In my blood.

We are zealous for perfection;
Yet none can be found
In the noisy halls
Of my heritage.

Machines
Ever buzzing
Overwhelm the serenity
In these boxes of conformity.

But if we slide open the door
And let the cold hit our senses
We might be transfixed
By the heavens
Full of stars
And endless water
Cascading over the edge
Of time itself.

If we might only step away
If we might only step away

We can hear it.

THE SHADOW

I hate what I've become
I am a shadow
With no form to rest
Let alone
A place to
Lay myself.

I am a wind
And a wave
Which chills others to the core
Just for my very being.

This tightness won't release
From the whole of me
This weary vessel
Cannot find hope any longer
In a space too cramped
For life to thrive.

I see it for others
The whole world even...

But not for me.

Not for me.

If you could hold me
Until I slip away
At least ill know
That I had shape once
That once upon a dark lit night
I was something
Resembling
Human.

THE SERPENT'S TOUCH

I can't stand when he touches me
It feels like lies of the skin
Deception
Wrapped in the flesh
Of a tender touch turned foul.

I curl up in a ball
Like a wounded dog
Resigned to his fate

How can one not know?

I cringe
And my greatest strength
Is needed
To not dissolve into weeping.

How is that not truth?

I cannot explain to anyone
The predicament
I am in.
They would not believe it.

I hate that touch
Yet it is meant for love
How has it come to this?

I cannot breathe
In the worst possible way.

My tears must fall silent tonight.
Tomorrow I will strain again
To try to give them voice

THREE STANZAS IN A NIGHT

A week ago this evening
You taught me how to dance
In-between my two worlds--
I'd like another chance

A week ago this night time
I knew we were alone
I rested as I never do
For your arms are my home.

A week ago this moment
I watched you fall asleep
And I held on tight beside you
For only the memory could I keep.

THE FOLLIES OF OUR YOUTH

I fight to live outside the abyss
But I realize
Every time
I think I see water
It is just a mirage.
The only place
To drink
The life blood of humanity
Is over the ridge
Where I fear to go.

People have told me
It was evil
It was a place
Never to even speak of
Ne look at
Or dare travel to.

Yet it is my only option left.
My one remaining
Place of hope.
And I am dying of thirst.

I am afraid to go,
For perhaps it is as terrible
As others have claimed
But I know I cannot stay
For the air is dry
And the sun is hot
And I have young ones to care for.

DRINKING INIQUITY

I would rather drown in the flood of my iniquity
Than live in the desert
Of expectation.
The dry land
Scorches me.
And all others see the oasis
All others know how water tastes
But I
Carry the ring
Of loneliness.

I would rather walk tall
And naked
Than clothe myself
In the garments of lies,
In the tapestry
Of tailors
Whose
Fabric makes me ill.

I would rather cease to breathe
Than sip the
Vapors of this humid
Earth
That paupers
have created around me;
The rich men who pillage and burn
As they go.
And the whole world
Is collateral damage
For their pocketbooks.

I would rather rest in the eye
Of sinners
Than have the righteous brand me theirs
For I know I am none;
And nor are they.

I dress myself in blood.

The blood of the crying land

The blood of youthful perceptions
The blood of the king
Risen again
with the strength
That now powers me.

I would rather dine in the excrement
Of the untouchables
Than feast
On the table of manufactured
Gravel and grit
Spray painted
For my deception.

For I am made of human stuff
And my human stuff; god sees that it is good.
And I can thus do no more
Than stand.

GO HOME SAINT GENESIUS

The wind blows upon my fortitude
And the justification
Of fire and flame
Cannot
Be quenched by
Words alone.

I ache
Inside and out
Trembling
With the cycled
Functions
Of who I am.

Who am I?
I am nothing
But a particle in the wind
Passing by
The streams
And rivers
And varying pathways
Of the world.
I am but a whisper
Carried from tip
To crest
Of every passing wave.
The waters never cease.

I do not care for
The boxes and lines
Of our world.
They yield no purpose to me.
They yield no fruit
For the work of my sewing.

I fear I am too heavy for you.
My thoughts
Are as guided
As an avalanche
And I do not wish to lose you
In my tremors.

You.

Special you.

Special you.

These guiltless
Rantings
Turn me no where else
But where the wind still carries me
Conveniently
Eastward.

I have no home.

I now understand what the epistles mean.

COUNT DOWN TO MY DEATH

I'm empty.
I am no use to anyone
I am simply a burden.

I always knew I was different.
Why couldn't I have been like my brother and sister?
They even look the same.

I am a curse to those who know me.
And a reprehensible leper
To those who don't.

I cannot hide it anymore.

All the masks have been burned
And all that remains
Is my grotesque form.

Therefore I chase god like a
Lightening rod
And pray he still listens... And acts.

My whole life god has said "wait"...
I'm beginning to question if I will simply become the tin man—
frozen in my gaze to nothing.

I am not a nihilist, but my oldest friend
Answers only in riddles.
The Yoda of the creation
Of all time...

Perhaps the birds can give me what I need, for i fear if they cannot
I may forever lose my joy in the melody.

I AM YESTERDAY

In the late night hour
My craft rears
It's cryptic head
And the dark masters
Of my thoughts
Tend their fires.
So long I have left alone the various parts
Of my madness;
Leaving it in listless words on a page
Or sounds up to heaven;
But now I have an ear.

A soul stepped forward
And chose to listen.
So I write.
So I strain my ear
To hear the refrains
Of callous voices
Echoing a familiar
Threat.

There is no tomorrow.

There is no yesterday.

Time is a manifestation
Of our fleeting imagination.
The clicks of your
Piece
Are your master.
You slave to hit marks
And values
And permits
Within its scope--
And fight
With all your might
And cleansers
It's rugged flashings
On skin
And bone.

Rust.

We all rust.

Our hearts harden and decay long before our visage
Is cleansed of all it's
Unwelcome views.

Lusty and false,
I lay here.

What is your purpose?
What is mine?

The clock strikes
And the chimes remind me of my futility.

But still,
You read my musings
So even the deepest parts of me
Perhaps
We're not born in vain.

STOPPING IN THE WOODS ON A DRY AFTERNOON

I lay quaking
Beneath
The shadow of who I once was
And though the role
Had been called
For all other wretches
Of the earth
And stewing more
Come join me-
There is none other to come forward.

I am alone in my crooked path, and the brush
Has thickened
Since last this walkway
Was tread.

There is a soft song of a bird
And distant roarings
Of a civilization
Somewhere beyond
The river.
But they are not here,
They are not me.

A rusted gate bars my going forward,
But the teeming crowds
Prevent my retreat--
So I am lost in the overgrowth
Praying for another soul
In this green desert
To show themselves...

Sometime it was you...

So I close my eyes,
Desperate to find
Respite
From the hoards.

And I search for you

But you are not there--

And I know, deep in my soul, that it is not my place to
Beg you stay;
Though my wretched spirit craves it.

And the wind drifts past,
And the buzz of a foreign world
Hums to and fro--

But my only chance for solitude is to turn my loneliness

Into a blessing.

MINNEHAHA

A bright light beams through the front glass and sun cascades around
the frame of
A young girl as she ascends
The stair
And a pair of eyes catch her.

It is a momentary fortune
Captured in
those same hallways,
The very classrooms,
Where began
my tutoring
On how
To hide in plain sight.

But months and years and decades pass
And the stories that transpire in
Between
Fill the void of that space.

Lives wander
And start
And end
Before those two fellows ever speak
And the dialogue of ages
Was passed through the lips of others
Before the phrase
"Do you even know who I am?"
Was uttered.

There are whole lifetimes lived
In a single sentence;
And moments that we cannot escape from.
Some things rapture like an accident
And others echo
As meant to be
From the windy caverns
Carved from the very breath of those
Who've come before.

I dare not say your name

Or it will become
A curse word
Upon his lips,
Another reminder of my sinful nature.

I dare not breathe your thoughts
Else he decipher what drives my glances.

You are now my secret.
Like a broken participle of the weighty traction that my life has become.

The air is always heavy and thick in this dirty part of ourselves

But a small girl once noticed
The blonde little duckling of her teacher
In that open expanse

And though mountains have moved
And ash has sifted into the seas
The children are still present
And the memory still pressing
In the heart of them.

THE MUSE OF FIRE

My muse
You are beginning to haunt my thoughts
And dance around in my brain
Like a runner
At the finish line;
Such joyful exuberance you bring.

My pulse quickens
At the thought of you;
When I see your light
Shining my way.

I feel something happening in the cosmos.
Planets and stars are moving in the heavens
And hope is swelling
Inside the tides of my heart.

OPUS TO THE LIGHTENING

Have you ever felt at one with the world?
The whole world?
It was beating
And you were beating
And it was alive
With you?

The whole world…
Beating with your drum
Even as you danced to theirs
And we all know the world is just
People
Just people,
Lavish and frustratable
But the glory of that moment!
Every knee bowing…
It was perfect
We were singing
To a thunderous tune

We were all singing together
And the lights were there broadcasting their
Fury to the electric company.
And the rains crashed down
And the water set us free
We were dancing
And the storm chasers beyond wanted in
To be one with us:
The world.

Have you ever sung a tune with everyone that ever lived?
Have you ever sung
And heard their echoing refrain?
It's amazing
The thump
And the grump, slump, bump…

Have you ever danced the airwaves
To your friends

Across a pool of
Cascading children?
Turning your tricks…

I used to melt into the envy of my own self
Dancing….
Singing….
With the
Whole
Freaking
World.

It was amazing, wouldn't you agree?
Let's do it again.

I danced with the world,
The whole world
ah! Can you see it?
Can you feel it again?!
We were smushed together
In the wet and rain,
Dancing,
And you said
I didn't need so much space,
I could share a little

We were all just there,
Trying to dance…
Trying to sing...
Just there, trying to be…

and our creator looked down and
Cried
Great tears
Of joy…

THE TAPESTRY

There is so much pain
In the corners
Of the fabric
Of the world;
And we are woven together
With such an acrid
Tapestry
That our bindings cut
And the melding of our sutures is often buckled and frayed

So the weaver tightly winds the joint with twice as much thread
And despite our efforts to tear apart
The seamstress still knits us together
And we are forcibly pulled
This way
And that

And blue does not like red

Nor orange, pink
And the menagerie of our promised land becomes a frozen patchwork
Of anger
And retribution
And we cry from our inner cores
Yet manifest in anger
For we no longer trust
Our yellow and purple and brown and plaid
Neighbors with our hearts
Our wounds
Our cherished memories
Of bicycles
And apple trees
And running through the carven stones
Of a hotel for the dead

And so we skulk along with each other
The nylon string like a shackle
And our tied frames of silk or wool or burlap
Simply want to rip away

And become a hankie for an elderly woman
Or a cloth to wipe the communion font

But our weaver will not allow the seems to rip
Nor the strings to stress
And every so often
The bearer of our collective
Coat
Is a child
Eager, quiet, sweet
And he wraps himself in us...

And we can no longer fight against each other
For the child cannot be warmed by the torn tatters of the parts
But needs the collection...

So we find our common purpose
And the child pulls snugly our sinews around his neck and
Makes himself superman
Or clutches us close with hot chocolate after a cold winters season...

And we might forget for a time that cashmere is too refined to be sewn
in with flannel; and even though denim is for the poor, the weaver
For some inexplicable reason
Crocheted it in with
Egyptian cotton...
So we forget
and in that forgetting we remember

We are only useful together
We only have purpose together
For if we can then one day
We too might realize that there is no child holding us
But we are
In fact
Simply holding each other.

WHAT YOU'VE DONE

My poetry is terrible.

I blame you.

My mind cannot choose any words
Worthy
Of what you are.

I mean to write.
I mean to convey
The flutters of my heart
And the wistful
Murmurs of my body
To the page
So that all can know what you do to me.

But words do not suffice;
And even if they could
My brain has such little energy
To muse on them,
For most all of me
Dwells on you.

Your strength
And humility
And energy
And joyful presence.
Your character
And tenacity
And humor.

You bring such a powerful electricity
To this sphere
Of our tiny existence
That all my systems fry.

Overload.

You overload my circuits.

My poetry is terrible

I blame you.

You've stolen my vocabulary
Just as
You're stealing

My heart.

WHEN FIRST I LOOKED AT SUNSHINE

I don't know you

      But I want to

I don't see you

      But I want to

I close my eyes
And the world is a different place.
It is a place where dreams come true,
And love can be fulfilling,
And children can play
Where is no threat of violence
Or retribution.
I feel your breath on the wind
As It's blown north
From the confines where you keep yourself;
I close my eyes
And I can hear your voice
And the harmony
I've searched for
Can be mine.
Could be ours
I close my eyes...

You don't know me

      But I wish you did.

You don't see me

      But I wish you could.

I close my eyes
And the subtle refrain
Quenches the tears of my parched eyes.
Heartache
Like ripples in a pond
And I am the stone.

I don't know you...

But I want to.

I want to.

OF TIME AND QUAKING

This abyss of time
Has no bottom.
No foot hold
Or place to lay your head.
There are no stop gaps,
Only manufactured moments.

Is it any wonder we give children
A graduation
So that
They can, perhaps,
Feel as though they've done
SOMETHING?

The longer you breathe
The more you feel
That world around you.
You either feel it
And know you are a part of it's hubris
Or shut it out
With walls
And laws
And religious exemptions;
All in an effort to purify
Your lungs
From the exhaust
Of your own
Wasted
Efforts.

All is a decay.

The light is dying.
The world is dying.

Why do we so focus on pain?
Why do we so try to manage trauma?
It is as inevitable
As the setting sun.

I was young once
And dreamed
Of that
Utopia
Where songs are sung daily
And the water is cool to the skin;
But now I have grown
And seen how
The balance sheet
Of life
Is no
Algebra equation.

Real life
Is not as simple as
Mathematics
Would have you believe.

The sink hole of time
Takes a ladder to cross
A ladder dragged down
Into our personal
Darkened caves of memory;
And only one traveler
May traverse
Per trip.

Alone.

Ever alone in the dark.

I wait for you on the other side.
Your voice comes to me in my weakness
In my dreams;
And I can still remember
The flaxen color
Of your golden locks
And the way
Your penny whistle
Sounds
During drinking games.

I wait for you...

And wonder--

How long, how long can my pupils last...?
If my eyes have nothing to gaze upon
Will light ever penetrate them again?

How does mankind put action to the word 'hope'?

THE SHAPE OF YOUR SMILE

The shape of your smile is becoming difficult to recall
And the melody of your voice is but a fading echo in the hollow of my
ears

I wish it were not so
For soon I fear you would disappear
Entirely.
Yet
You've painted a picture
In the inner parts of me,
One whose colors my soul cannot forget;
You have etched yourself
Onto something eternal
Which ever flows with bursting hope

But oh...
My hands and my heart do wish
That my darkened eyes
May once again see
By the light of your face
And yours
And yours
Alone

THE LONELY HEART

Tears come swiftly
To a body
Ready to break
To a mind
Willing to quake
And a life
Preparing to crack.

There is a loneliness
In the raindrops
Where serenity
Once sat.

It's that familiar bedfellow
One that was a common partner
Until the groundhog
Saw his shadow.

But though 6 weeks of winter
Miraculously
Turned to twelve
Even the groundhog
Could not
Stop
The coming of spring:
That ironic spring
Where hope dies
And the millstone claims it's victory.

The cracking thunder warns of greater fire
And wind
And redemption
Yet to be burned to

And the shattering earth
Is no great matter.
The masses do not even notice;
For it is only a single heart
That has fallen.

AND ON AND ON…

I live in a relaxed time

A time of commentaries
A time of visionaries
And ability
To muse on the working of the world.

It is a privilege to be a poet
that has been earned on the backs of my forebears

it is a privilege to be a pauper
broken by the weight of impoverished masses
who strive
for what I've been given unjustified.

it is privilege to be a pilgrim
to make my presence known
out of the shadows when I choose

Will you let me wade through your memories
and tiptoe through your life?
I will not leave a mark,
just perhaps a ripple…

It is just a jester's footprint, never lasting past the laughter…

It is a privilege to be a passerby
losing life into the enormity
of the sea
quietly drifting while not a structure is stirred…

not even you…

I promise I won't stir you,
unless perhaps,
my ripples
get hold of
                    the wind.

ABOUT THE AUTHOR:

Becka Thompson is an actress, mathematician, teacher and writer. In her spare time she runs marathons and teaches her son the jedi arts. She is an alumna of both the Juilliard School, where she is a proud member of Group 31; and also the University of Minnesota, where she proudly got a BS degree.

She lives in Minneapolis with her family.

www.ingramcontent.com/pod-product-compliance
Lightning Source LLC
LaVergne TN
LVHW011410080426
835511LV00005B/464